SPORTS & FITNESS

how to use your body and mind
to play and feel your best

by Therese Kauchak Maring
illustrated by Brenna Hansen

with Caroline Silby, PhD, sport psychology

★ American Girl®

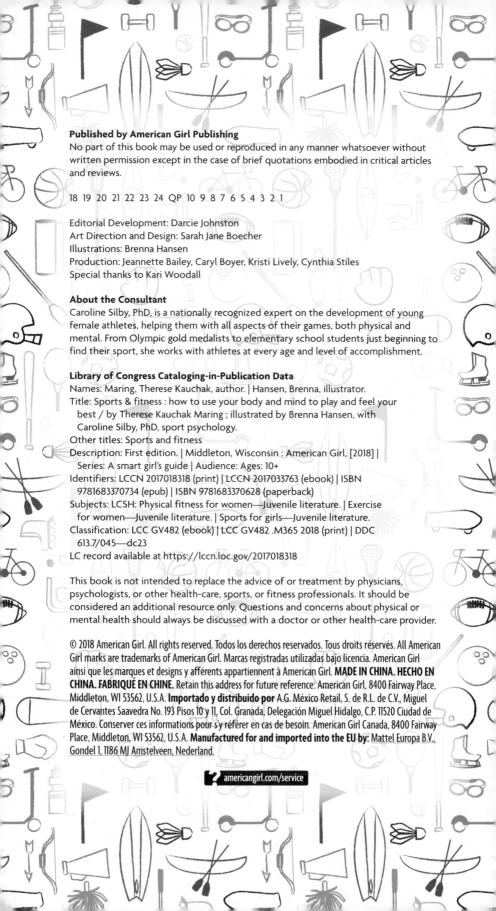

Published by American Girl Publishing

18 19 20 21 22 23 24 QP 10 9 8 7 6 5 4 3 2 1

Editorial Development: Darcie Johnston
Art Direction and Design: Sarah Jane Boecher
Illustrations: Brenna Hansen
Production: Jeannette Bailey, Caryl Boyer, Kristi Lively, Cynthia Stiles
Special thanks to Kari Woodall

About the Consultant

Caroline Silby, PhD, is a nationally recognized expert on the development of young female athletes, helping them with all aspects of their games, both physical and mental. From Olympic gold medalists to elementary school students just beginning to find their sport, she works with athletes at every age and level of accomplishment.

Library of Congress Cataloging-in-Publication Data
Names: Maring, Therese Kauchak, author. | Hansen, Brenna, illustrator.
Title: Sports & fitness : how to use your body and mind to play and feel your best / by Therese Kauchak Maring ; illustrated by Brenna Hansen, with Caroline Silby, PhD, sport psychology.
Other titles: Sports and fitness
Description: First edition. | Middleton, Wisconsin : American Girl, [2018] | Series: A smart girl's guide | Audience: Ages: 10+
Identifiers: LCCN 2017018318 (print) | LCCN 2017033763 (ebook) | ISBN 9781683370734 (epub) | ISBN 9781683370628 (paperback)
Subjects: LCSH: Physical fitness for women—Juvenile literature. | Exercise for women—Juvenile literature. | Sports for girls—Juvenile literature.
Classification: LCC GV482 (ebook) | LCC GV482 .M365 2018 (print) | DDC 613.7/045—dc23
LC record available at https://lccn.loc.gov/2017018318

americangirl.com/service

Dear Reader,

From the time you were little you've been playing. After you took your first steps, you figured out how to run. As you got older, you learned how to roll a ball, ride a bike, do a cartwheel. You made the amazing discovery that if you tried, your body could do new things, learn new skills.

One day, you were old enough to play organized sports! Soccer, T-ball, karate, dance—moving your body was still fun, even if it was a little more complicated. There were rules, harder skills, teammates, and coaches to figure out.

By now, you've grown and can do things you'd never have thought possible a few years ago. There may be a sport (or two) that makes you feel special and strong—or that fills you with joy. At your age, sports aren't quite as simple as they used to be, but if your brain and your body are pre-pared, they can be just as fun.

This book shows you how to be the best athlete you can be, in both body and mind. You'll find ways to keep your body strong and learn skills that can help you improve, no matter what sport you play. You'll learn how to harness your brainpower to deal with nerves—or anything else that gets in your way. You'll also get expert advice to help you do and be your best in tough situations.

Being fit feels good, and it's good for you—whether you play an organized sport or do something solo, whether you play casually or seriously. We hope that by the final pages of this book, you're eager to keep on playing, trying new things, and having fun!

Are you ready? Let's play!

Your friends at American Girl

contents

play power 7

what's so great about sports?

body bonuses

brain bonuses

life bonuses

Quiz: why do you play?

your body 19

fuel up!

your game-day plan

hydrate

be prepared

training dictionary

warming up

on the injured list

trainer's tips

sports Q&A

power drills . . .41

be stronger

last longer

be more agile

hand-le it

challenge course

sports Q&A

your mind 59

train your brain
Quiz: take charge
get set, go!
parent traps
sports Q&A

brainpower skills 73

pre-game
during the action
after the action
Quiz: are you a good winner?
Quiz: are you a good sport?
sports Q&A

you & the team 89

team sports or solo spirit?
you say
all for one
got spirit? let's hear it!
10 ways to be a leader
sounds like trouble
coach talk
coaches' corner
sports Q&A

go for it! 109

you're a champ!

I love so
many sports!

I like
ballet, jazz,
and tap because
I get to dance my
heart out . . .

and I like swimming
because floating feels
awesome and it lets me
have quiet time . . .

and I like tennis because
it's good exercise and it
makes me feel alive . . .

play power

and I like volleyball
because it feels so great
to hit that ball!
—Alisson

and I like soccer because it
gives me a chance to run in
the green grass . . .

what's so great about sports?

Chances are, if you're reading this book, you already like playing a sport—or doing something that works your body and keeps you fit. So why do you do it?

Maybe you play because you love to run, shoot hoops, kick a ball, or do back handsprings— because it just feels great!

Maybe you think *any* kind of moving is more fun than sitting still or staring at a screen.

Maybe you like discovering your body can do things you didn't know it could do.

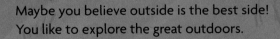

Maybe you believe outside is the best side! You like to explore the great outdoors.

Maybe you play sports because you like being part of a team . . .

. . . or because it's fun hanging out with your teammates. *Hellooo,* pizza parties!

. . . or because the feeling you get when your team accomplishes something together is like happy-times-10!

High five! Those are all great reasons. And that's not even all you get when you play.

IMPORTANT!

Before doing any of the exercises described or shown in this book, check with your parent, coach, doctor, or other appropriate adult to make sure it's right for you, your body, and your sport.

9

body bonuses

You play because it's fun! But that's not all. Playing sports also sets you up to be healthier for your whole life.

It helps your bones.

Bones are made of living cells. When you do weight-bearing exercise, new bone tissue is formed, and that makes your bones stronger. Any sport is weight-bearing if your legs support your body weight while you move. So when you're walking, running, jumping rope, dancing, or playing soccer or basketball, you're building strong bones.

It helps your muscles.

Well, duh, right? If you play sports, your muscles get stronger. That's Sports 101. But what does that really mean? It means you don't get tired as quickly when you play. And the stronger your muscles are, the better they are at protecting you when you're moving. That means you're less prone to certain types of injuries, both on and off the field.

It helps your heart.

Exercise that gets your heart pumping and makes you breathe hard is giving your heart a workout, too. Your heart is a muscle. And the stronger it is, the better it is at pumping blood to your lungs and the rest of your body. More oxygen and nutrients get to your tissues. You're heart-healthier, and you have more energy.

It helps your ZZZs.

This one's simple. Experts who study fitness say exercise can help you sleep better, and a well-rested you is a happier, healthier you.

How much exercise do I need?

Health experts say girls your age should get at least an hour of physical activity every day. If you play sports, practicing and competing will get you to an hour on many days. Gym class counts, too. So does recess and walking the dog.

As part of that activity, you should do something that gets your heart pumping for at least 30 minutes three times a week. Those 30 minutes can be two 15-minute or three 10-minute bursts of activity. You'll get the same health benefits as an all-at-once 30-minute workout.

What kind of exercise is best? Anything that's so fun it makes you want to play! In fact, experts who study fitness recommend that you don't pick just one sport to specialize in. Playing multiple sports is best for your body.

It helps your future.

You haven't met Grown-Up You yet. But if you keep playing sports, you're going to like her when you do. Not only will Grown-Up You be fun to hang around with, she'll also be healthy and fit. Playing sports now means you're more likely to be active as an adult.

brain bonuses

You play because it feels good—starting with the thrill of the game. But sports and exercise also feel good in ways that might not seem so obvious.

☑ MORE self-confidence

When you have fun playing a sport, you feel good about yourself. Whether you're scoring the goal, making a solid pass, or cheering from the sidelines, mastering a skill makes you proud. It can help you realize you're capable of doing other amazing things, too.

☑ LESS stress

Does it seem weird that playing in a real nail-biter or doing a hard workout can reduce your stress? It's science! It happens because exercise can reduce the levels of hormones in your body that are related to stress, such as *adrenaline*.

☑ BETTER moods

Exercise stimulates the production of brain chemicals called *endorphins*. Endorphins are known as "mood elevators" because they can help you feel happy, optimistic, and less depressed. It's like pushing a button for your brain to take an elevator to a happier floor. It's the science behind why a walk, swim, or bike ride can get you feeling up.

☑ BETTER concentration

Remember how your pumping heart is increasing the blood flow throughout your body? The blood is pumping to your brain, too, and that can make your brain function better. Some research shows that exercise activates the *hippocampus*, the part of your brain that's important for memory and learning.

☑ IMPROVED performance at school

Researchers have found that girls who play sports often do better academically. And because you're sleeping better and concentrating better, you may also, in turn, be getting better grades.

☑ MORE time to chill

Some exercise helps you relax because of the kind of activity you're doing. Maybe you like the solitude of walking the dog or the peace of canoeing with your big sister on a quiet lake. Some people get their best thinking done when they have fewer distractions. Worries about friend drama, school, or your busy schedule just fade away. *Ahhh!* Peace and quiet, inside and out.

13

life bonuses

You play sports because you like to! It feels good to play, but more than that, you're picking up skills that can help you off the field, too—now and for the rest of your life.

You learn that you can deal with life's ups and downs.

In sports, you know you may win . . . or lose. You keep going, even if it's hard. That's called *perseverance*. You learn to look back at a loss and find things about your performance that were "wins." Knowing that who you are is not decided by what happens during one event can help you at school, at home, or at work someday.

Being able to bounce back when things don't turn out as you'd hoped— that's called *resilience*. It makes it easier to deal with new situations and bumps in the road your whole life. You know that the challenge might be easy—or not—but either way, you can keep moving forward.

You learn people skills.

In sports, you play with loud people, quiet people, goofballs, and serious types. You learn how to cheer them on and support them if they're down. You learn that if you speak up when you don't understand, things will make more sense. You learn there are good ways and bad ways to disagree.

Being able to empathize and being good at communicating and resolving conflicts will make you stronger and more independent wherever you go. These skills make you a leader!

14

You learn that you can learn.

Picture yourself playing your favorite sport. You may not remember, but there was a day when you'd never played it before. You had never, say, kicked a soccer ball—ever. But look at you now: You have skills! You learned a few things and then a few more. You're still improving. Throughout your life, you'll always need to learn—whether it's skills for your career . . .

> I need to fix this Mars Rover, stat!

. . . or to understand what's going on in the world and solve problems.

> As president of the United States, here's what I think . . .

As an athlete, you understand it's OK not to know everything at first, because you can learn. That translates to confidence and bravery.

You learn to handle pressure situations.

Races, games, matches—in sports, competition can equal excitement. There are bound to be pressure-filled situations, like when your team is down by one in the ninth inning and you're up to bat.

In solo sports you take on pressure, too. Imagine you're surfing: You see the perfect wave forming, and you're trying to position yourself to catch it before it's gone. You learn it can be fun to conquer a challenge.

That doesn't mean you'll never be worried or nervous. You learn to recognize nerves, take a deep breath, and face the task head-on. And a girl who's ready to face a challenge with gusto instead of fear will go far.

Quiz

why do you play?

Stop and think for a minute about why you like to play sports, whether it's a team activity or something you do on your own. Which of these sound most like you? Pick all the answers that apply.

I like to go all out!

Playing in games is exciting!

My teammates are my best friends.

I found out I'm good at this, and I can accomplish things.

It takes my mind off other things. When I play, I focus on the game and everything else goes away.

My sisters all play volleyball, so I do it, too.

I like that I get more time with my friends.

It makes me feel graceful and creative.

I love being outside.

My dad says it makes me more well-rounded, and that it could help me get into a good college.

It's better than sitting inside all winter!

It makes my mind quieter.

I like learning new skills.

I feel like my teammates have my back, on and off the field.

My family says I need to do at least one physical activity every year.

When I accomplish something, I feel like, YEAH!

I thought it might be a little scary. But I like the feeling when we're in a close game and then we win.

Scoreboard

You may play because it's **fun** or because it makes you feel good. You may play because it strengthens your friendships or because you find out new things about yourself along the way.

If your answers show you might be playing for **reasons that aren't your own,** dig deeper. Can you think of two or three things you enjoy about playing? Did it take a tiny push to get you started, but you like it now? How often do you come home from practice or a game with a smile on your face? If you can't come up with positive answers to these questions, this book will help you find a solution—or find the fun!

I love being in the water because my body feels so free, like I can do anything!
—Abby

I love being active. It makes me feel healthy and beautiful.
—Josephine

your body

Playing sports is fun,
and it makes me feel
awesome about
my body.
—Cali

fuel up!

As an athlete, you ask a lot from your body. It's important to know how to treat it well and keep it energized, healthy, and ready for action—starting with what you put into it.

Food is fuel.

To stay strong, you eat right. And the more you move, the more you need. So refuel regularly to keep your body performing at its peak. If you spread healthy meals and snacks through the day, you won't run out of gas!

Every body needs the vitamins in fruits and veggies. And dairy foods like milk, cheese, and yogurt are loaded with calcium for strong bones. You already know that.

Do you also know how important carbohydrates and proteins are? Carbs store fuel inside muscles—so you want your tank full of them before you play. Protein? It gives you energy, helps you grow and recover from exercise, and builds strong muscles. It's actually what muscles are made of!

Some good carbs

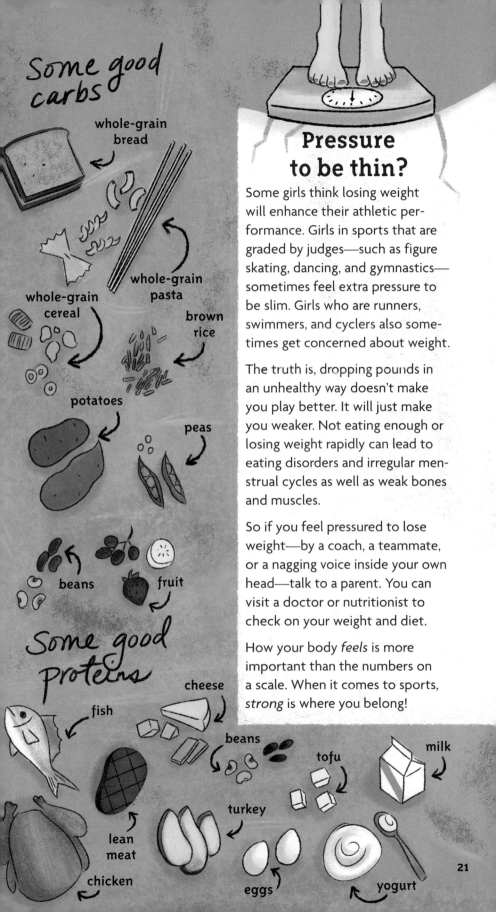

whole-grain bread

whole-grain pasta

whole-grain cereal

brown rice

potatoes

peas

beans

fruit

Some good Proteins

fish

cheese

beans

tofu

milk

lean meat

turkey

chicken

eggs

yogurt

Pressure to be thin?

Some girls think losing weight will enhance their athletic performance. Girls in sports that are graded by judges—such as figure skating, dancing, and gymnastics—sometimes feel extra pressure to be slim. Girls who are runners, swimmers, and cyclers also sometimes get concerned about weight.

The truth is, dropping pounds in an unhealthy way doesn't make you play better. It will just make you weaker. Not eating enough or losing weight rapidly can lead to eating disorders and irregular menstrual cycles as well as weak bones and muscles.

So if you feel pressured to lose weight—by a coach, a teammate, or a nagging voice inside your own head—talk to a parent. You can visit a doctor or nutritionist to check on your weight and diet.

How your body *feels* is more important than the numbers on a scale. When it comes to sports, *strong* is where you belong!

your game-day plan

Psst! Here's a secret strategy tip. On game day, eating right can help you have more energy and perform your best. Experts who study nutrition recommend **these tips** and food options for game day.

Don't skip breakfast.
Wake up your body and start the day right with a full tank.

BREAKFAST

★ healthy cereal and whole-wheat toast with eggs, yogurt, or milk

★ smoothie made with fruit, yogurt, and milk

★ oatmeal with milk and berries

★ egg sandwich on whole-grain bread (bonus: spinach leaves!)

Lunch

Eat lunch, too.
If your game starts right after school, lunch is extra important!

★ turkey in a whole-wheat pita with lettuce and tomato, plus an apple and yogurt

★ vegetarian? peanut butter on whole-wheat bread with carrot sticks

Have a healthy snack.

Snacks are your secret weapon on game day!

SNACKS

- ★ veggies and hummus
- ★ string cheese and an orange
- ★ trail mix
- ★ peanut butter crackers
- ★ granola bars or fig bars
- ★ low-fat yogurt with fruit

Don't get greasy!

Cheeseburgers and pizza taste great, but they can slow your digestion and make you feel tired. Save them for the after-party!

Time it right.

It takes 2 to 3 hours for your body to digest a meal, so it's best not to feast right before you play. Eat a solid breakfast and lunch, and have a small snack up to 30 minutes before playing.

Replenish at dinner.

Dinner is the chance for your body to recover after the big event. Include carbs in the evening to help you prepare for tomorrow's action.

DINNER

- ★ whole-wheat spaghetti with meat sauce, veggie salad, milk
- ★ baked potato stuffed with bean chili, broccoli, carrot sticks, milk

hydrate

When you exercise, you sweat—sometimes a little, sometimes a lot. It's important to replace the fluids in your body by drinking water all day long, whether you're exercising or not.

What does water do?

Water keeps your body temperature constant so you don't overheat. It carries good things like oxygen and nutrients to your cells and carries out waste products. It helps lubricate your joints—picture the Tin Man in Oz before Dorothy uses the oil can. And that's just the beginning of the list!

How much water do I need?

It depends on your age and weight. On average, a girl between the ages of 9 and 13 needs to drink about seven 8-ounce cups of water a day. When you're exercising, drink small amounts of water before, during, and after. Don't wait until you're thirsty to drink.

Can you handle some toilet talk? One place to tell if you're hydrated enough is the bathroom. If your urine is pale yellow or clear, you're good. If your urine is dark yellow and there's not much of it, you need to drink up. Here are some guidelines:

About two hours before you exercise:	Drink two to three cups of water.
About five to ten minutes before you exercise:	Drink one cup of water.
While you exercise:	Drink about one cup of water every 15 to 20 minutes.

If it's especially hot where you play, drink a little more.

After you exercise:	Drink more water to rehydrate after you've been sweating.

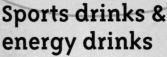

Sports drinks & energy drinks

Skip the hype. Water is the only hydration that most girls need.

★ Sports drinks and vitamin waters usually contain ingredients that replenish your body after a tough workout. But they often pack extra sugars, which you don't need.

★ Energy drinks are different from sports drinks. Energy drinks have caffeine or other ingredients marketed to "boost your energy." These drinks are unregulated and can be dangerous for young athletes.

★ Protein drinks or powders may sound good because, as you know, you need protein. But experts who study this say you're probably getting all the protein you need through the foods you eat.

★ Chocolate milk is a popular recovery drink with adult athletes who do intense forms of exercise. For girls involved in normal practice and game situations, though, it's not necessary.

Stick with water, and you'll be made in the shade . . . or the sun!

25

be prepared

Stay safe by heading to each practice and game prepared for success. Following these safety tips can help you get the most out of your performance and prevent injury.

Play it simple.

Remove necklaces, bracelets, earrings, and rings before you take the field.

DANGLE = DANGER

In many leagues, if you're caught wearing jewelry, even by mistake, you're disqualified. It's always safer to leave your fashion accessories at home.

Protect yourself.

You probably know if your sport calls for protective equipment such as a helmet, mouth guard, face mask, goggles, shin guards, or other pads. This isn't your first rodeo, as they say. (Or in your case, maybe they say karate match or cyclo-cross race.)

But last season's gear doesn't do much good if you've grown two inches. At the beginning of the season, ask a parent or coach to check the fit of every piece. If you have a growth spurt during the season, check again! Wear all the equipment that's required, and be sure it fits right.

Dress for success.

In cold weather, wear layers that can be peeled off as your body warms up. In hot weather, light colors will keep you cooler. Your shoes don't have to be the most expensive brand in the store, but to prevent injury, make sure they fit well and are right for your sport. If you're not sure, ask your coach.

Be sun smart.

If you play a sport outdoors, protect yourself from the sun. Wear a hat or cap whenever you can at practice and games. Check with your coach about the rules for game attire.

Apply sunscreen on all exposed skin—face, neck, arms, legs, and the tops of your feet if you'll be barefoot. (Use an SPF lip balm, too!) If sunscreen bothers your eyes, apply it from the cheeks down and keep your hat on. Don't forget to cover your ears and the back of your neck, and reapply often if you're swimming or sweating. Read the labels, looking for a product that offers "broad spectrum protection" against both UVA and UVB rays. Your sunscreen should have a Sun Protection Factor, or SPF, of at least 30.

If possible, avoid being outside in the middle of the day, when the sun is at its most intense. Choose shade whenever you can!

training dictionary

You hear a lot of
fancy terms around
the gym and at practice.
Here's a guide to help
you learn the lingo.

abs

back

obliques

glutes

hips

Your body's abilities

AGILITY

the ability to change your direction and increase speed without losing control.
To improve your agility, your coach might have you zigzag through cones or hop through a ladder shape that's marked on the floor.

ENDURANCE

the ability to exercise for extended periods of time.
The better your endurance, the longer you can last before you get tired. With a little effort and the right exercises, everyone can improve her endurance!

CORE STRENGTH

the strength and power of the muscles in the middle— or core—of your body.
Core muscles help you do everything from standing up straight to powering your arms and legs through swings and kicks that are both powerful and safe.

FLEXIBILITY

the ability to move your muscles and joints through their full range of motion.
You may be more flexible in some areas of your body than in others. Flexibility training focuses on healthy ways to stretch, and it keeps you ready to move.

BALANCE

the ability to hold your body position and not lose control.
It's more than hopping on one leg without falling over! When you work on balance, you learn to engage your core muscles to hold your body steady in all directions. That can make you stronger and protect you from injuries.

MOBILITY

how well your body can move properly and safely.
Mobility depends on flexibility, strength, and the condition of muscles and joints. Imagine a toddler squatting to pick something up off the floor. So easy! Then picture an elderly person doing it. The difference is mobility!

Training terms

Cardio or cardiovascular training: exercise that raises your heart rate and quickens your breathing. Also called *aerobic training*, it strengthens your heart and improves endurance. Basketball, biking, jumping rope, running, skating, soccer, swimming, and tennis are just a few examples of good cardio workouts.

Interval training: an endurance-building workout in which you switch between bursts of quick, powerful exercises and lighter movements. For example: Walk one block, jog to an upcoming tree, and repeat. *High-intensity interval training (HIIT)* uses more powerful exercises during workouts, such as full-out running instead of jogging.

Plyometrics: exercises where you repeatedly stretch and contract your muscles to increase power. Also called *jump training*, examples include skipping, hopping, and leaping. A plyo program can improve your muscles' ability to stretch and power back, like a rubber band!

Resistance, strength, and weight training: using your body to push or pull to build muscle strength. You might do push-ups or pull-ups, where the weight you're moving is your own body. You might do moves using a medicine ball, or you might stretch wide rubber bands in different directions. Besides strengthening muscles, weight-bearing exercise also strengthens your bones.

Suspension training: exercises that use your own body weight, gravity, and suspension equipment to increase strength, balance, and mobility. Two straps with handles on the ends are suspended from a secure point. By holding on to the handles and adjusting the angle of your body and the length of the straps, you can work different muscle groups.

Extra-credit classes

Don't know your barre from your boot camp? Here's the what's-what on classes you may see at a fitness studio.

Barre class: exercises involving a hip-high rail attached to a wall, inspired by the way a dancer works at a ballet barre. These exercises can improve your posture, flexibility, and core-muscle strength.

Boot camp: a high-energy class—named after a military training course—that focuses on working all your major muscle groups. Classes can be hard but fun, because you and the other boot-campers are all in it together!

Pilates: movements that strengthen your core muscles and improve flexibility, endurance, and coordination. Some moves are done sitting or lying on the floor, while others require special equipment found at a fitness studio or gym.

Rolling: floor movements that involve lying and rolling on a foam cylinder to massage out tight spots in your muscles. Also called *myo-fascial release*, rolling can help you recover from certain injuries.

Yoga: poses (also called *asanas*) that can reduce stress, quiet your mind, and build strength, balance, and flexibility. You may be familiar with some poses, such as downward-facing dog or child's pose. The full practice involves moving through poses in combination with breathing techniques.

Remember this:

It's always important to have trained instructors guide you in any form of exercise that's new to you.

Monday Tuesday Wednesday Thursday Friday

warming up

Before you jump full-speed into practice or a game, your body needs to get ready. These exercises will warm you up—and get your mind and body firing together.

Warming up may seem easier than the workout or the game, but athletes know it's just as important. Be sure to think about what you're doing rather than simply go through the motions. A key part of warming up is being connected mentally to what your body is doing.

Start with a 3- to 5-minute cardio warm-up. **Walk** briskly or take a relaxed jog down the block and back.

Jog down the block and back again—but this time work in 5 **butt-kicks,** where you try to kick your glutes with your heels as you run. Jog some more regular steps, and then do 5 more butt-kicks. This continues to warm up your body temperature. It also increases your heart rate and the blood flow to your muscles.

Warm up your hips, starting with **up-and-outs.** Jog 5 or 6 steps and stop. Lift one knee forward and up, and then rotate it out to the side. Set your foot down. Jog 5 or 6 more steps and repeat with your other leg. Continue until you've done 5 lifts with each leg. Walk back to your starting point, and go through the cycle again.

Reverse the leg motion and do **up-and-ins,** continuing your hip warm-up. Jog 5 or 6 steps and stop. Lift one knee up and to the side, and then rotate it to the front of your body. Set your foot down. Jog 5 or 6 steps and repeat with your other leg. Continue until you've done 5 lifts with each leg. Walk back to your starting point, and go through the cycle again.

To prepare your body for sideways motion, **step side to side** in place for 30 seconds.

Add **arm circles** while stepping side to side. With your arms straight out to the sides, make small arm circles, gradually increasing their size. Circle forward and backward for 30 seconds each.

7

Do gentle **shoulder rolls** while jogging in place. Raise your shoulders up toward your ears, and then roll them back and down. Repeat 10 times. Then roll in the opposite direction—up and forward—10 times.

8

Do the **Frankenstein with a twist.** Stand with your back straight. Step forward with your right leg and gently swing your left leg up in front of you while reaching toward it with your right hand. Don't kick hard—it doesn't matter how high you raise your leg. Gently twist your head and shoulders toward the side with the raised leg.

Lower your arm and leg, stepping forward as you go. Then raise the opposite leg and arm. Continue stepping, gently kicking and twisting as you walk forward. Take 5 steps with each leg.

Check with your coach for other warm-up moves tailored for your particular sport.

on the injured list

OUCH!

Sooner or later, almost every athlete gets some kind of injury, big or small. It's no fun, but it doesn't have to stop you completely.

Overuse injuries happen when your body doesn't have the strength to deal with the same physical stress over and over again. This kind of injury often happens in sports like tennis and cross-country running, where certain muscles get a lot of use. Specializing in only one sport and playing it year-round can also lead to overuse injuries.

Acute injuries result from a sudden impact or misstep, like spraining your ankle during a soccer game. With an acute injury, you might be out of the game for four to six weeks.

Sometimes just *lifestyle* can put an athlete at risk. Too much stress—from balancing a tough workout schedule with school, or from dealing with pressures of competition—can leave a girl's body in less than prime shape to perform. And that could lead to injury. If you find yourself feeling extra moody, unable to sleep, or slipping with schoolwork, you may need to take a break.

No pain, no gain?

Listen to your body. Sure, working hard in sports means sore muscles and minor aches here and there. But remember, pain means something. If you have mild to moderate pain for more than two weeks, see a doctor. And if the pain is severe, get help immediately.

Now what?

If you do get injured, don't give up or worry about being left out. Keep your head in the game, even if your body can't be, and find other ways to be on the team. When your body heals, your mind will be ready to take the field.

These tips will help you avoid injury—*and* help take you from good athlete to great!

Take time off.

Your body needs time to recover. Take at least one day off per week, and at least one month off per year. Explore a variety of sports or activities instead of focusing on just one.

Start right.

If you're not in top shape when the season begins, start slow and increase your workout gradually. Follow the 10 percent rule. Each week, increase your training time, the distance you cover, or repetitions of an exercise by just 10 percent. For example, if you start out by running 20 minutes a day, the next week run for 22 minutes.

Stay flexible.

Tight muscles are more prone to injury. Follow your coach's warm-up program, and remember to stretch during cool-down sessions after exercise.

Try strength training.

Strength training can decrease your risk of injury by making your tendons, ligaments, and bones stronger.

RICE ADVICE

A sprained ankle is one of the most common sports injuries. If it happens to you, remember RICE!

Rest: Avoid using the sprained joint or putting weight on it. Stay off your ankle as much as possible.

Ice: Apply an ice pack to shrink swelling and ease pain. Go for 20-minute increments—20 minutes on, 20 minutes off—and do this 4 to 8 times a day for the first 48 hours or until the swelling stops.

Compression: Wrap the sprained area tightly in a stretchy elastic bandage to keep it stiff and protect it from further injury.

Elevation: Keep the sprained joint raised on a stack of pillows to help reduce swelling.

Sports smarts: Knee & head injuries

Experts who study sports are becoming more aware of *ACL tears* and *concussions* in girls.

ACL stands for *anterior cruciate ligament*. The ACL helps protect your knee when you slow down while running, land from a jump, and pivot or cut. For girls, ACL tears are most often seen in soccer, basketball, and gymnastics. Coaches can recommend a training program that includes plyometrics and strengthening exercises, especially for core and lower leg muscles. A coach may also spend extra time teaching proper technique for cutting, pivoting, and landing when you jump.

A concussion happens when someone's head or neck is hit hard enough that her brain knocks against the surface of her skull. With girl athletes, concussions usually happen from contact with a ball or another surface, not another player.

A concussion can have long-term effects, so take any head injury seriously.

If you've hit your head or have any of these symptoms, stop playing immediately and let your parent or coach know.

Concussion symptoms

feeling sluggish, hazy, foggy, or groggy

nausea or vomiting

double or blurry vision

sensitivity to light or noise

balance problems or dizziness

drowsiness

just not feeling right or feeling down

concentration or memory problems

headache or "pressure" in the head

confusion or feeling disoriented

SPORTS Q & A

My knees hurt every time I play basketball. My dad took me to the doctor, and she says I need to take a break for two weeks! What am I going to do without my team and practice?

I can't believe I broke my wrist! I have a cast on my right arm from my knuckles almost to my elbow! I won't be able to play volleyball for months, and even when my bones are healed, it will be a while before I'm full strength. I can't even ride my bike around the neighborhood.

Answer

Injuries can hurt mentally as well as physically, because they prevent you from being able to do what you love—play! The good news is, the injury is only temporary. And part of becoming a great athlete is learning to deal with forced time-outs like these.

Injuries can be a great time to re-charge your body and mind. It's called *active recovery.*

★ Keep moving the healthy parts of your body. If your arm is injured, for example, get on your feet and take a walk.

★ Keep going to practices and games to stay connected to your teammates. Offer to help your coaches set up drills or run the warm-up. Give your teammates positive feedback and encour-agement. Spreading enthusiasm will keep *your* spirits lifted, too.

If you'll be on the sidelines for quite a while, use the time to explore things that can help you when you're back in action.

★ Learn about *mindfulness,* a tech-nique that can help you relax and calm jittery nerves. Ask your parents to download an app for mindfulness or deep breathing, and spend 10 minutes a day learn-ing these new skills. Mindfulness can help you with homework overload, friend stress, and test worries, as well as when you're back playing sports.

★ Before you go to sleep at night, try doing a mental rehearsal. Close your eyes and imagine yourself playing your sport bet-ter than ever!

Answer

It can be hard to get used to wearing clothing for sports that you would never wear to school. But chances are, others aren't noticing how your leotard looks. To them, it represents your athleticism. It's tight so it stays put as your body flips and spins through the air. And it's like a bathing suit so you stay cool while working up a sweat.

You've earned that leotard! Wearing it shows you've reached a certain level of commitment to your sport. When you're with your friend, avoid talking about your appearance and instead focus together on the fact that leotards make it easier to train.

Think, too, about what's really important—the traits that make you a good gymnast and your friend a good dancer. Those include things like the effort you put into practice, your spirit, and how well you listen to and learn from your coaches.

You may feel self-conscious. But if you surveyed 100 people, it's likely none of them would be thinking about what you're wearing! They would be too busy watching in amazement as you glide across the beam or as your friend pirouettes across the floor. Treat your body kindly. After all, it's protecting some extremely special gifts—including your strength, your abilities, and your dreams!

FLIP for Gymnastics

STRONG is Beautiful

The more I practice
and stretch, the higher
I can kick and the
better I can do.
—Hannah

I love how my body
can twist and bend
and swing.
—Dena

power drills

I exercise every day, whether it's doing push-ups or dancing to music.
—Kate

I love my very strong legs.
—Bethany

 # be stronger

Power up! You don't need fancy equipment to become stronger, faster, and sharper at your game. Just add some some basic power drills to your practice, and your skills will get better and better. Turn on the tunes— and have fun!

Polished plank

Experts who study fitness recommend you do muscle-strengthening activities at least three days a week. One good way to improve your strength is to practice *plank position,* which works your core muscles. Your core is called your "powerhouse" for a reason. With strong core muscles, you're a more powerful, stronger you in almost every way.

To know what it feels like when your core muscles are working, place one hand on your stomach. Now clear your throat or cough. Feel how your muscles tighten? Some coaches call that "engaging" or "activating" your abdominals. That's the feeling you'll want your core to have during plank.

To begin, position yourself on hands and knees in *tabletop position.* Your hands should be directly below your shoulders. Make your back flat and your hips even, not tilted one way or the other. If a cup of water was placed on your lower back, it wouldn't spill. Look down at your hands— not back at your knees or up at what's in front of you.

Timely tip

Most cell phones have a stopwatch setting you can use to time yourself. Set your phone up where you can see it—but not step on it.

2 Fire up your muscles! Tuck your toes under. Squeeze your glutes, and engage those abs. Slide your shoulder blades toward each other and down toward your waist. Straighten your elbows and *squeeeeze* your armpits, like there are invisible sponges under your arms and you want to wring out every drop of water. You're activating all those muscles!

3 Now lift and then straighten your knees, and—*ta-da!*—you're in a powerful push-up position. That's where a strong plank begins. Imagine a straight line from your head to your feet, so your butt isn't raised in the air. Push gently through your heels, and hold for 10 seconds. Relax. The day when you can do that easily, add another 10-second hold. As you get stronger, keep adding 10-second holds until you can do six in a row.

Options

⭐ Planking on your forearms instead of your hands is just as challenging! This is sometimes called *hover* or *elbow plank*.

⭐ From plank or hover, raise one foot an inch off the ground, hold it for several seconds, and lower. Repeat on the other side. It's not about how high you raise your foot. It's about how still you can keep the rest of your body while you do it.

⭐ Planking with a friend? Position yourselves with the tops of your heads toward each other, looking down, with about 6 inches of space between you. Once you're in plank, raise one hand slowly (keep your hips straight), and give each other a low five. That's teamwork!

The key with all your planks is to maintain a powerful, active pose and keep your "tail" from wagging. Good job!

Eyes and chin down, Badger!

Supergirl

It's important to strengthen the front *and* back of your upper body. If your muscle strength isn't balanced, you're more likely to be injured. Plank strengthens the front of your body. To strengthen your back, fly like a superhero. Bonus: This strengthens your core, too!

1 Lie facedown on the floor with your arms extended forward. Keep looking down toward the floor throughout the move.

2 Tighten your core muscles, and lift your right arm and left leg off the ground a few inches. Hold for about 3 seconds, and then relax and prepare to switch sides.

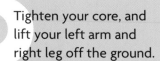

3 Tighten your core, and lift your left arm and right leg off the ground.

4 Try for 10 times on each side.

Lunge time!

Lunge exercises strengthen all the muscles in your legs: the quadriceps (or quads, the muscles at the front of your thighs), the hamstrings (the muscles running along the back of your thighs), the calves, and the glutes, too!

There are lots of ways to lunge! To do this simple alternate-leg lunge, start with your feet together.

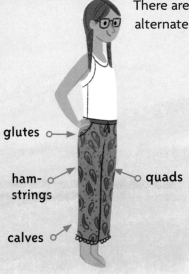

glutes

ham-strings

quads

calves

1 Step forward and lower your back knee toward the ground—that's a lunge. **Important:** Your knee should be bent at a 90-degree angle. That means your front knee should be right above your ankle and should not extend beyond your big toe. Keep your back straight, and don't lean forward.

2 Pushing down on your front heel, straighten the knee of your front leg so you're standing again. Then move your front foot backward to starting position. That's one! Keep your core muscles active the whole time.

3 Repeat with the opposite leg.

4 Work your way up to 10 lunges on each side, alternating legs.

45

last longer

Jumping rope might be the perfect way to build endurance, helping you last through long games and tough matches. It's easy and it's fun. It works your lower and upper body. It helps your coordination. And it's weight-bearing, so it even strengthens your bones. Experts who study fitness recommend bone-strengthening activities at least three days a week. So hop to it with these drills!

Jump start

1 Start out jumping for 2 minutes. Use a two-footed bounce, which means both feet landing at the same time.

2 Over the next few weeks, work your way up to 4 minutes.

 When you can jump for 4 minutes straight, move on to these interval-training drills that go from slow to fast speed and back to slow again.

Bunny hop

3 Then slow down for 1 more minute.

4 Repeat this sequence for a total of 2 to 4 minutes.

1 Start with 1 minute of steady, regular jumping. Use a two-footed bounce.

2 Next, without stopping, speed up for 15 seconds.

Speed up your jump-rope jog for 15 seconds.

Skip or jog with the rope, one foot landing after the other. Jog 5 steps forward and 5 steps backward. Continue for 1 minute.

3 Now go back to a slow jog for 1 more minute.

4 Repeat the whole cycle for a total time of 2 to 4 minutes.

On the first jump, land with both feet together. Keep your knees flexed and your weight on the balls of your feet.

On the next turn of the rope, spread your feet about shoulder-width apart.

Repeat, alternating together and apart, for 1 minute.

4 Speed up for 15 seconds, then slow down for 1 minute.

5 Repeat the whole cycle for a total time of 2 to 4 minutes.

47

be more agile

Ready, set, move! These drills work on your agility, helping you change direction quickly, increase speed, and maintain your balance. Do them on a gym floor or a dry, hard-surfaced driveway or playground. If you're inside, use masking tape to mark off the plus sign and ladder shape. If you're outside, draw the shapes with chalk.

Plus sign

Mark off a 4-foot-by-4-foot plus sign on the ground. Number the squares 1 through 4, like in the illustration.

Begin with both feet in square 1. Jump diagonally, using both feet at the same time, to square 4 and back again to 1. Repeat for 30 seconds. Count how many jumps you can do in that time.

Rest for 30 seconds. Now switch to the other diagonal, jumping from square 2 to square 3 and back. Repeat for 30 seconds. Count your jumps.

Done with diagonals? Jump forward—from 3 to 1—and back. Then jump sideways—from 3 to 4—and back. Do 30 seconds of each, and rest for 30 seconds in between.

Have a friend time you, and record the number of jumps. In which direction do you jump the fastest? Keep working on your speed, and it will improve. Put in the work, and you'll see the results!

Ladder

1 Mark a ladder on the ground that's 5 squares long. Each square should be 18 inches by 18 inches.

2 Stand at the beginning of the ladder with your back straight, your knees slightly bent, and your weight on the balls of your feet.

One in the square

3 Starting with your left foot, step into the first square and jog through the ladder, one step in each square. As you jog, keep your steps light and your feet as low to the ground as you can. Let your arms help power you! Pump them—don't let them hang by your sides.

4 When you reach the end of the ladder and step out of it, scoot around the outside and back to the beginning. Do "one in the square" two times.

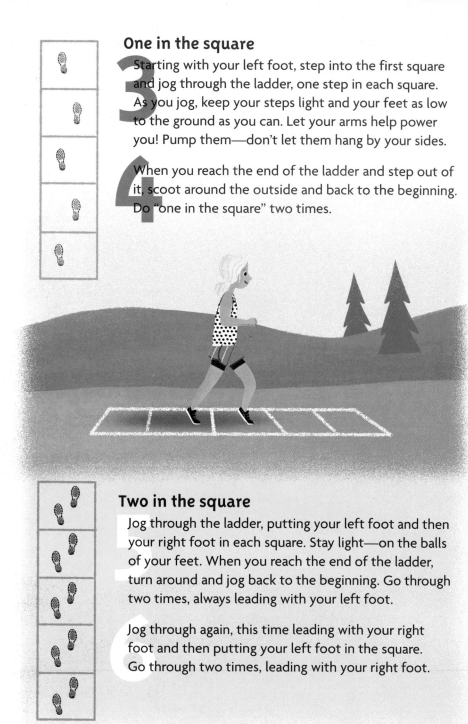

Two in the square

5 Jog through the ladder, putting your left foot and then your right foot in each square. Stay light—on the balls of your feet. When you reach the end of the ladder, turn around and jog back to the beginning. Go through two times, always leading with your left foot.

6 Jog through again, this time leading with your right foot and then putting your left foot in the square. Go through two times, leading with your right foot.

Do the ladder several times slowly before gradually speeding up. It's more important to move with a nice, steady rhythm than it is to race through! Most of all, pay attention to your body position: straight back, bent knees, and weight on the balls of your feet. Start with good form on basic ladders, and eventually you'll climb up to more complicated steps. Ask your coach if you're ready for more!

Tree pose

Balance is an important part of agility. With good balance, your body stays stable. That means you move more efficiently and are less likely to get injured.

1 Stand on two feet. Squeeze your glutes and tighten your core muscles. Carefully lift one foot up to rest on the inside of the other leg. You can rest your foot low on your calf, or higher up, above your knee. Do what's comfortable, and use your arms to steady yourself.

2 When you're ready, slowly raise your arms over your head. Don't worry if you tip. Finding your balance again is part of the exercise! After a few seconds, lower your foot to the ground. Take a deep breath and exhale.

3 Now try it on the other leg.

If you feel wobbly, use a "kickstand"—keep the toes of your raised foot on the ground and rest your heel above your other ankle. Or stand with your back against a wall for support. Once you've mastered that, move on.

51

hand-le it

Want to have the quickest hands around? A tennis ball is your secret weapon for becoming better than ever at throwing and catching with either hand.

Popcorn ball

Play outdoors or in an open gym where there's plenty of room. The key is to keep your eyes on the ball. Watch it all the way into your hand as you catch it.

1 Stand about 6 feet away from a wall. Gently toss a tennis ball overhand at a spot on the wall a few feet above your head. If you need to, catch the ball with both hands. Repeat several times.

2 Next, throw and catch the ball a few times using only one hand.

3 Then toss the ball with one hand, but use only your fingertips to lightly catch it and quickly toss it back.

4 Now throw the ball with one hand, and catch it with the other. After a while, try it with opposite hands. Keep practicing, and you'll get better with each toss!

Juggling

Juggling is a great way to improve your hand-eye coordination. You learn to work with both your left and right hands, and you improve your balance, too!

Start by juggling a large, light scarf that will float slowly in the air when you toss it. Then move on to beanbags and light juggling balls.

Online videos are a great place to find juggling tips and ideas! Ask your parents to help you find some.

challenge course

Bring out your inner warrior! Design a just-for-fun course that brings together all your skills. Set up stations with the equipment you need at each one. To mark the end of your course, cut out a red circle from construction paper, and tape it to a wall or tree—that's your finish-line buzzer. When you're ready, turn on some music, and you're off!

Station 1
Do 10 jump-rope jacks.

WOOO! HOOO!

Station 8
Touch the finish-line buzzer—and do a celebration dance!

Station 7
Go across monkey bars, if you have them. If you don't, grab your jump rope again and do 10 more jump-rope jacks.

Station 6
Bounce a tennis ball. Holding a tennis racket with your elbow bent at the waist, bounce the ball straight up 10 times. Don't let it hit the ground!

Station 2

Do 10 rotations with a toy hoop. Try to keep the hoop going, but if it falls to the ground, just pick it up and keep at it until you've tallied 10 twirls.

Station 3

Hold plank for 10 seconds.

ONE, TWO, THREE...

Station 4

Balance in tree pose for 5 slow, deep breaths.

Track It

Have someone time you as you make your way through the course, and keep track of your personal best.

Station 5

Bear-crawl for 10 steps.

GROWL

When you bear-crawl, your knees don't touch the ground. Start in plank position, and turn on those core muscles. Stay on your hands and the balls of your feet, bringing each knee up toward each elbow. Try to keep your butt down and your bear tail from wagging side to side.

55

My friend and I were on our very first soccer team together. Now that we're older, our skill levels aren't the same. We tried out for a more competitive team, and I made it, but she didn't. What do I say?

Answer

Part of the wonder of sports is that no two journeys are exactly the same. There's one thing you and your friend will always share: You'll both experience victories and losses—just not necessarily at the same time. You can stay connected by honoring each other's good times and disappointments.

Part of becoming a great athlete and teammate is knowing how to elevate others—that is, showing your friend how she shines. You can still talk about your games and how your seasons are going. Be happy for her when she does well. When she has disappointments, remind her of her strengths and what you admire about her.

Remember that the sport choices you make—and those made for you—will help you create your unique story. You and your friend can embrace how your stories are both alike and different. And if you ever end up playing together again, that will be another special chapter.

Answer

In sports, you learn the biggest lessons when you move outside your comfort zone. Challenging yourself to try something new can be hard or scary at first. But you can be proud of taking a shot to see if you'd like a higher level of play.

Our hockey club has different teams for my age. One level is more competitive and is for more advanced players. It sounds exciting, but I'm not sure about it. How do I know if I'll like it?

When you face the unknown, you turn a worry into an experience. Dig deep to find your courage. You'll see that trying a new team can help you find out what gets you excited. And when you're having fun, you're ready to learn and improve. Even if the team is not a good fit, you understand yourself better—and that's a good experience, too.

> We have a traveling team and a regular team. I'm not sure if I want to be on the traveling team. Is that OK?

Answer

It's great that you have choices in the levels you can play. The most important thing is to *play!* It's absolutely okay for you to stay on the regular team—but it's important to understand what's driving your decision.

Before making a choice, identify your goals.

Are they to . . .	Or are they to . . .
• be with your friends?	• challenge yourself?
• get exercise?	• learn new skills?
• have fun?	• play with girls who are better than you?
• get lots of playing time?	
• be the star on the team?	• learn a new position?

Once you know your goals, you can ask your coaches and parents to help you determine which team is the best fit. Travel teams often require a big time commitment for games and training. They may prevent you from doing other activities you enjoy. On the other hand, travel teams can give you exposure to higher levels of play and coaching.

So which team is right for you? That depends on the goals and objectives you have for this sport, right now. Track your goals each season, so you can find the right team at the right time. Keep playing and having fun!

Confidence helps me play better
and helps my team win.
—Stella

When I play I feel happy,
and bad feelings just
move away from
my mind.
—Faith

I always feel good knowing
I tried my hardest,
no matter what happens.
—Bethany

your mind

Just focus on your goal and not yourself, then keep on working hard to reach it.
—AG Fan

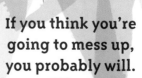

If you think you're going to mess up, you probably will.
—Tessa

train your brain

When it comes to sports, what's going on in your head matters as much as what's going on with your body. You already know that you need to exercise your body to play well. But how much time do you spend training your *brain*?

It's OK if you answered "not much" or even "um, none." Many people don't realize their thoughts are powerful tools and that healthy attitudes can be developed just like muscles.

Know you can grow.

Sometimes something you think is a fact . . . isn't. For example, you might believe:

I'm a pitcher. Shortstop is not for me.

I may be on the team, but I'm really not an athletic person.

I'm a sprinter. I run short distances, fast. I could never race a mile. Are you kidding?

or

or

When a thought like one of these runs through your head, you might think it's set in stone. But just because you have the thought doesn't mean it's true. It might be fear trying to disguise itself as fact. Learn to pause, and question the idea.

No one is *born* good at a sport—not even Olympic athletes. The best athletes get there because they have a *growth mind-set*. They started out as beginners at their games, and they gave themselves room to learn. Having a growth mind-set means you know you can always learn and improve.

It's OK to mess up along the way. Making a mistake doesn't mean you failed! It means you're trying. How good you become depends on how much effort you put into learning and becoming better. Knowing that you can grow is a powerful first step.

IT'S **OK** TO MESS UP.

I'M NOT AFRAID TO FAIL . . .
AND DO IT **BRILLIANTLY**.

I AM PERFECTLY **IMPERFECT**.

IT'S FINE TO BE SCARED.
I'M GOING TO TRY ANYWAY.

I KNOW I CAN **GROW**.

61

Claim your superpowers.

Sometimes athletes are so focused on fixing what they do wrong that they don't recognize what they're doing right.

For most girls, it's easy to describe in horrifying detail a time when they played badly.

I remember everything about it—how tired I was, the fight with Mom before the volleyball game, my first bad serve, the spike I hit into the net, the digs I missed. Then the long ride home and the black cloud over me the rest of the week. Ugh.

And remembering a time they played really well isn't too hard.

But ask them to name one specific thing they did that contributed to that happy moment . . .

Ummm . . .

and most people don't know. The truth is, you make the good things happen! You have super-powers that help you control the outcome of your performance. You just need to recognize them, and use them.

Think again about a time you felt really pleased with the way you played. Did you . . .

spend extra time practicing your serve that week?

ZZZ

go to bed on time the night before, so you were rested?

listen to music instead of fighting with your sister on the way to the game?

arrive at the game early so you felt calm instead of rushed?

tune out the crowd when you were on the court, listening to your coach and teammates instead?

trust your instincts and knowledge of the game?

focus on having fun?

Those actions are your superpowers. Make them part of what you do every week. You're not just showing up and watching from the sidelines as your life unfolds. You're using your superpowers to take control of your performance.

Find your pride.

Identify three moments during practice when you felt proud of what you did. Then write down one action you took that led to that good moment. For example:

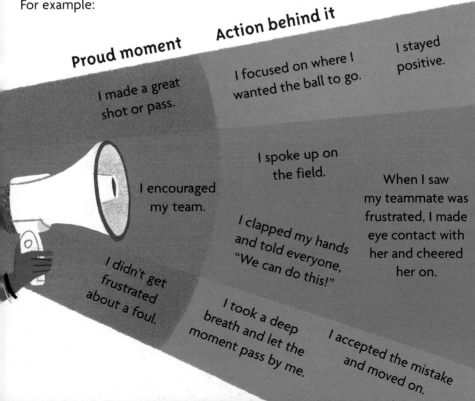

Proud moment

Action behind it

I made a great shot or pass.

I focused on where I wanted the ball to go.

I stayed positive.

I encouraged my team.

I spoke up on the field.

When I saw my teammate was frustrated, I made eye contact with her and cheered her on.

I clapped my hands and told everyone, "We can do this!"

I didn't get frustrated about a foul.

I took a deep breath and let the moment pass by me.

I accepted the mistake and moved on.

take charge

Only you control how well you play. It doesn't matter if the weather is sunny or dreary. It doesn't matter if your parents are there or if the crowd's on your side. If you let outside factors like these affect your performance, you're giving away control. It's as if you're riding a bike but letting someone grab the handlebars and steer you this way and that.

You can take charge of your thoughts! Try this quiz to see if you're in the driver's seat.

1. When I'm doing my sport, I don't dwell on what other people around might think of my moves.

   a. That's me.

   b. That's not me.

2. I know my parents will be happy with me even if I make a few mistakes.

   a. That's me.

   b. That's not me.

3. If an official makes a call that I think is bad, I don't let it bother me for the rest of the game. I shake it off.

   a. That's me.

   b. That's not me.

4. I'm just as calm doing my sport in front of a crowd as when no one is watching.

   a. That's me.

   b. That's not me.

5. It doesn't matter if the other team has a good record. Every game is a fresh chance to prove myself.

   a. That's me.

   b. That's not me.

6. I know there are things I can do to help me perform my best. Those are the things I pay attention to before, during, and after the action.

   a. That's me.

   b. That's not me.

Scoreboard

In the driver's seat

If you had more **That's me** answers, you know that how well you play and how hard you try are things that you control. You don't let other people's expectations get you down. You roll with the punches when something bad happens. Good going!

Time to take charge

If you had more That's not me answers, remember that outside events don't affect how well you play unless you let them. During the game, concentrate on what you're doing, and forget what others think or how the crowd is reacting. If an official's call goes against you, don't dwell on it. Focus on what you can do: play your best! Read on to learn more strategies for doing just that.

get set, go!

The competition's about to begin, and your body feels a rush of jumbled emotions . . .

Your heart races.

Your stomach flutters.

Your palms sweat.

Believe it or not, those nervous, eager feelings are good things. They come from a substance called *adrenaline* that pumps through your body. Before a game, your body is a little like a can of soda that's been shaken up. The adrenaline is bubbling around inside you, making you feel edgy. When you start to play, that energy is released, like the liquid that fizzes out of the can when you pop it open.

You can keep jitters under control by recognizing them as normal reactions your body is having. They're not a sign that you're scared or that you're about to make a mistake.

You know you're prepared. You can handle anyone who comes your way. Your body is saying you're ready to move. You've got the power—and you can use it!

Fight or flight

A funny thing happens when you get into an exciting or stressful situation playing sports. Your body doesn't know if you're about to run a race or be run over by stampeding elephants. It just knows you're feeling anxious, and it gets you ready to take the challenge (fight)—or take off (flight). Your pre-game nerves are your brain getting your body ready to act.

Here's how the fight-or-flight response generally works:

Your brain tells your adrenal glands to release adrenaline into your blood.

Adrenaline produces the changes your body needs to react. It makes your heart beat faster to pump more blood to your large muscles—which means it's moving blood away from your tummy.

That's the butterfly feeling you get in your stomach!

So when your heartbeat speeds up and you feel a little jumpy, recognize those feelings for what they are instead of being freaked out by them.

It also sends sugar and fat into your bloodstream as sources of quick energy. And your body heating itself up and cooling itself down is what's making you feel clammy or sweaty. Those are all good things.

Oh, hello. It's you again. LET'S DO THIS!

Remember those feelings are normal, caused by your body getting you ready to move. They're not signs that something's wrong—so don't avoid the action in the game or overthink the situation. Trust your body. Trust your training. Trust your game plan, and go for it!

parent traps

Most adults want to be supportive when they watch their kids' sporting events. But sometimes their words and actions send a different message, which can be distracting during the game. Here are **some behaviors** you might see.

Bragging

Maya has been winning awards since she was two.

Spotlighting

Grab the ball, Sameen! Take it! You're a winner!

Come on, Lianne, you're better than that!

Pressuring

Hey! What do you mean FOUL? No way!!

Arguing

Blaming

The refs are dopes, and the field's a mess! No wonder we're losing.

When it happens to you

Just because you see grown-ups behave this way doesn't mean it's right. It's not the only way to act, and it doesn't have to stay this way. Don't let distractions from parents get in your head and keep you from having fun or playing your best.

When tempers flare

It can be embarrassing or even scary when adults lose control. If your parents' behavior bothers you, find a quiet time and tell them how you feel. Stay calm and let them know you understand they are trying to help, but their words and actions are doing just the opposite—they hurt. Try saying . . .

> I saw you were really mad in the stands. When you yell at everyone like that, it's not fun for me.

> Maybe you could talk to them after the game and not yell.

> It would help me more if you gave me playing advice at home instead of on the field.

> What I'd like most to hear you say is, "I love watching you play."

Coach credit

Be sure your parents have the full picture of what your coach does for the team. Does Mom know Coach helped you one-on-one at practice this week? Does Dad know Coach videotaped your swing and how patient she was reviewing the video with you? Tell them. If your parents know the good things your coach does, they might appreciate her more and understand that your coach is usually on your side.

MISSING IN ACTION

Maybe your parents aren't there at all. Often parents have good reasons for missing games, but if it happens a lot, it can hurt.

Let your parents know how much their presence at games would mean to you. They might think you like having them out of your hair or that staying away lightens the pressure to perform well. If having them in the crowd would make you feel confident and proud, say so.

My parents like to give me advice, but it's different from what my coach says. Both my parents are good athletes, so I think they know what they're talking about. I just want to play the best I can. What do I do?

Answer

You're not alone—almost every athlete has experienced this! Your parents and your coach all want you to play well. But "play well" may mean one thing to your folks and something quite different to your coach.

Your parents may think you played well today if you scored. Your coach may think you played well if you executed a certain move better than you did last week—even if you didn't score. Because they have different definitions of playing well, they're giving you different advice.

On the field, the coach is in charge. You need to follow the coach's game plan. At home, ask your parents to help you consider how their advice and the coach's instruction might fit together, like puzzle pieces. If your parents don't believe the coach is giving you proper instruction,

encourage them to speak directly with the coach. It can help your parents understand the coach's philosophy and be sure that this team is the right fit for your skill level and your goals.

You can also talk with your coach to be sure you have a clear understanding of what's being asked of you. Even if it's confusing at first, these discussions can help you better understand the game and the different ways that goals can be met. That's a good skill to have for your whole life.

During games, my dad yells at my coach. He cheers against players on the other team. He questions the referee's calls all the way from the bleachers. I want to play the game and have fun. But sometimes when I hear his voice I just want to disappear.

Answer

It is definitely easier to focus on the game when spectators show respect for the rules and for your opponents.

Let your dad know that the "noise" from the bleachers affects how well you play and how much you enjoy the game. Maybe invite him to shout encouragement rather than criticism. That way he gets to show his enthusiasm and help you keep your focus on the field, where it belongs.

Each time you get distracted by noise from the stands, bring yourself back to the action. Take a deep breath and exhale, like you're blowing the noise away. Smile at a teammate, and remind yourself that you have her support. Tense and release your thigh muscles as a way to let out any physical tension you're holding.

In the end, you can control only your own behavior. And as long as your body is out on the field, your head needs to be there, too!

When I get called for a foul, it's hard not to take it personally. What can I do?

Answer

If you get called for a foul, it shows you are playing aggressively. That means you play hard and are willing to give it your all to help the team.

So don't let a foul bring you down. When the whistle blows, instead of getting angry, think about your physical contributions to the team—your shooting, passing, or whatever skills are appropriate in your sport. Then recognize your emotional contributions—your risk taking, hard work, and dedication. Those are some positive facts you can take personally! **71**

In bed at night, I imagine
my body flowing perfectly
through the moves.
—Rosina

My team is always laughing
together, so even when we
lose, it feels like a win.
—Zoe

brainpower skills

When I'm playing my best, I feel so determined.
—Flannery

It doesn't matter if I win or lose, because I can always beat my personal best.
—Rachel

pre-game

When it comes to performing your best, your mind is as important as your body. You've been training your brain to think positive. Now it's time to learn techiques for thinking *smart!*

For starters, during practice and before the action begins, the key is to shake off frustrations and get yourself ready for success.

Easy as a-b-c and 1-2-3

Sometimes before a game, when your brain is looking for something to do that will get the result you want, it turns to worry. Your brain thinks . . .

What if (scary thing 1) happens?

Or what if (scary thing 2) happens??

Or what if (scary thing 3) happens?!?

A mental game called Counting the Alphabet can help you *pivot*, or turn away from the worry. It keeps your brain active and turned on but calms the balls of anxiety bouncing around in there. Do it before the game to clear away anxious thoughts. Bonus: You can also do it at practice or during a game if you're frustrated about something happening on the field.

Here's how. When the worry starts, hit pause. Then count the alphabet, like this:

1A 2B 3C
4D 5E 6F
7G 8H 9I
10J and so on …

That's tricky to do, especially when you're antsy. And that's the point! Counting the alphabet keeps your mind working—but it helps take your mind off whatever is frustrating you. It makes you *pivot*. Count to 10— or longer if you need to. Then move on!

Strike a power pose

Changing your body language can change what's in your head. Think about how you hold your body after you win or perform well.

Compare that with how you hold your body when you're nervous.

head up

eyes down

shoulders back

shoulders hunched

arms crossed

standing up straight

feet apart

You feel strong, you feel tall, and you feel open. You feel big! Some call this a *power pose*.

You pull into yourself. You might separate yourself from your team. You feel small.

Experts say that putting your body in a power pose can help you feel stronger and more confident, and get your brain ready for a good performance. So while you're on the sidelines waiting for the action to begin, stay open and big. Practice your power pose!

75

Imaginary moves

If you watch figure skaters on TV, you've seen them getting ready before they go on the ice, moving through their routine on dry ground. They're wearing headphones, listening to the music of their program, imagining each leap and spin in their mind's eye. They're *visualizing*.

you can do it, too.

Start by doing a few jumping jacks to get your heart pumping like it does when you're in the action. Then close your eyes, and imagine yourself playing your best. See yourself making all the moves you've practiced. Smell, feel, and hear the environment, too!

If you're a swimmer, remember the chlorine smell of the pool, the feeling of the humid air, and the muffled underwater sounds of your stroke. See yourself exploding off the blocks, flipping through turns, and touching the wall at the end. Make the mental picture as vivid as you can. It's like watching a highlight film starring you.

Practice your mental rehearsal a few times a week, not just before a competition. That way, you're doing it when you're calm and quiet, not in the pre-game hubbub of a big event.

Watch this!

You can also watch videos of yourself and other athletes' great performances. This is a great way to visualize if you tend to imagine yourself messing up!

Crafty comparisons

When you think about your opponents before the game or when you see them face-to-face, your brain might click into comparison mode.

Make that work *for* you, not against you. Instead of worrying about the other team, think of a strength you have that balances your opponents' strength.

For example, they may be bigger, but you're fast. And you know your coach has a plan based on your team's speed and agility. Reminding yourself of any basic strategy helps.

Yikes! They're so tall!

Yeah, but we're *FAST!* And we're ready!

during the action

The thoughts you have during a game can affect how well you play. That's especially true if you allow a one-time mistake to mutate into a major problem in your mind. Practice these skills to stay relaxed when the competition is in full swing.

GO!!!! GET IT! YAY! BOO WOW! MISS! Slowpoke! WHAT?! HEY!! COME ON! WHOA. argh! SCORE! MOVE!

Tune it out.

The roar of the crowd is exciting—unless it gets in your head and distracts you. Athletes who have "rabbit ears" listen too closely to the cheers and critics in the crowd.

Don't let others get to you. Wherever the distraction comes from, use it to remind yourself of a simple action you can take. Think: *run fast, work hard,* or *eyes up.* This puts your attention where you want it to be.

Stay in the moment.

You've probably heard the phrase "eye of the tiger." It means staying focused in a fierce way, concentrating on doing your best *now,* at this moment. This. Very. Moment.

It doesn't matter if you had a false start in the last meet. It doesn't matter if your goal is to beat your biggest rival in next week's game. If you're thinking about what happened in the past or what might come in the future, you're missing what's going on here and now. Turn down the chatter in your head, and trust your body's natural wisdom.

Close the drawer.

Don't let a one-time mistake seem like a big-time problem. If you flub, imagine a tall dresser with many drawers. Open one of the drawers, toss in the mistake, and close the drawer tight.

You can't see the error anymore. It can't affect you, and it definitely doesn't determine how you'll play in the rest of the game. Lock the drawer, and throw away the key.

Get mentally tough.

Did you make a mistake because the other team was pushing you around? Your opponents know they stand a better chance of winning if they upset you. They want you to focus more on them than on the game.

If you refuse to get upset or to be intimidated, you take away their power. Play your game. Don't let your opponents get in your head.

Be a good teammate.

Friends make any challenge easier. On the field, your teammates are your support network.

But here's something really interesting: In a stressful situation, helping someone else can help you feel better, too. Your actions affect your own brain chemicals and can keep that stress cloud moving right along.

If you feel a dark cloud of stress arriving overhead, reach out and tell a teammate, "You can do this!" or "Good job!"

after the action

When the game is done or the action is over, welcome in positive thoughts.

Find the A's.

Is there a voice in your head keeping track of what you did wrong during the game? Knock out the negative! Instead, think of three things about your performance that you did well.

Come up with three "subjects" in which you can mark your report card with an A. Then find one more subject in which you're a B—something that with a little dedication and practice you can get an A in, too.

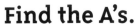

Listened to Coach A
Supported a teammate A
Made a good pass A
Hustled every time,
on and off the field B

Keep the desire burning.

When things aren't going as you'd hoped, it's normal to feel a little stressed. Remember that ups and downs are a natural part of sports.

Is it ever OK to quit?

Before you make any big decisions, take your emotional temperature: Do you feel a bit overwhelmed but in your heart know that good times are around the corner? If you think back on recent games and practices, can you still spot fun moments?

If so, then you're probably experiencing normal stress, and you can manage it. If the athlete part of you is feeling down, remind yourself of the whole person you are.

caring
friend

pancake
flipper

athlete

sister &
daughter

accordion
player

good
student

math
whiz

animal
lover

writer

What if you feel worse than that?

There's a bigger type of stress, called *burnout*. That's when it feels like things will never change, no matter what you do. You might feel exhausted, trapped, or not interested in your sport anymore. You might feel less confident, or feel sick and miss events more often. Maybe you feel like you've put *everything* into one sport, and you just don't know if it's worth it any longer.

What should you do?

Talk to your parents and coach. Sometimes burnout happens to athletes who focus on a single sport all year. More variety may help you feel better. Variety will also make you less prone to injury.

Try to reconnect with the good feelings you used to have. Instead of thinking about perfect scores and great stats, focus on *feelings* goals. Think about when you felt happiest playing your sport. What would it take to find those feelings again? You might need to play for a less competitive team, try a different sport, or take a break and do something else for a while.

> If you can get back to feeling free, powerful, and satisfied, you're on your way.

What's the final word?

When you join a team, you make a commitment to your teammates, your coach, and yourself. So quitting is a big decision.

Think it through. Give the activity, your coach, and your team a fair shake. If the season is short, play until it's over and then decide. If the game's still not fun, it may not be the sport for you. Try something new next season, and give it your all.

are you a good winner?

Are you as good in victory as you are in defeat?
What would you do in these situations?

1. Your team is way ahead. You're on the bench, waiting to get in the game. You . . .

  a. relax. You've got it made and want to let the other team know it! Does anyone want to have a bubble-blowing contest?

  b. get nervous. What if something bad happens and starts the team on a downward slide? What if you get in the game and you're the only one out there who doesn't play well?

  c. stay focused. The game's not over yet. If your team gets too full of itself, it might start making mistakes—and your opponents might get mad enough to come from behind and win.

2. It seems like you and two of your fave friends are the best athletes on the team. At the track meet, you three take the top places in almost every race, and your school wins. As you get on the bus, you say to the rest of the team . . .

  a. "Ta-daa! Here we are—the three-girl track team!"

  b. nothing. You just smile and look for a seat.

  c. "Good job, everybody! Way to work together."

3. Your teammate has had a rough day. She made some mistakes in her snowboarding event that left her embarrassed. It was her worst showing ever, and she seems discouraged. Afterward, you . . .

a. stay away from her. You don't want that bad luck rubbing off on you.

b. talk to her but don't say anything about how she played. You don't want her to think about her bad day.

c. say, "It's OK. Everybody makes mistakes. You're talented. You can do this."

4. Your team wins the game as the buzzer sounds. You . . .

a. screech over and over at the top your lungs, "Who's the best of all the rest? YAAAY US!"

b. congratulate your teammates, find your parents, and go home.

c. shake the hand of the opposing coach and every player on the other team. You say, "Nice game. Your team is really good. Great job out there."

Scoreboard

Too proud and too loud	Nothing ventured, nothing gained	Way to go!
If you answered **mostly a's,** you may come on too strong when you win. Don't let your pride in a job well done turn to arrogance. Think twice before you gloat about a victory or ignore a troubled teammate. Ask yourself, "How would I feel?"	If you answered **mostly b's,** you could give a bit more heart. Turn up the team spirit. Praise a teammate—or a competitor—who has played well. Lend an ear to someone who's had a bad day. The good you give to others—the way you elevate those around you—makes you a leader. And leaders are good competitors.	If you answered **mostly c's,** you're on the right track. You know not to get cocky when your team takes a lead. You share victories with your teammates rather than hog the glory. You always congratulate the other team, win or lose. High five!

are you a good sport?

There's no disgrace in losing—it's a natural part of sports. But how you handle yourself when you lose is as important as how you win. What would you do in these situations?

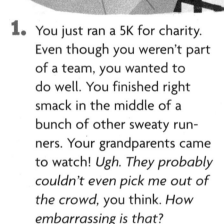

1. You just ran a 5K for charity. Even though you weren't part of a team, you wanted to do well. You finished right smack in the middle of a bunch of other sweaty runners. Your grandparents came to watch! *Ugh. They probably couldn't even pick me out of the crowd,* you think. *How embarrassing is that?*

a. Yes, that's me.

b. I might do this.

c. I'd never do this.

2. Your softball team lost, and you're really upset. After the game, you say to the coach, "Why didn't you let me pitch? You know I could've done better than Emma."

a. Yes, that's me.

b. I might do this.

c. I'd never do this.

3. You know you're a better swimmer than the girl who just beat you. But she had a better start off the blocks. You lean over the rope, shake the winner's hand, and say, "Congratulations, but I would have won if I'd just had a quicker start."

a. Yes, that's me.

b. I might do this.

c. I'd never do this.

4. Your teammate missed a basket at the buzzer that would have won the game. Afterward, you say to her, "Looks like you need to practice your layups more, Mia." You know it's good advice. She shouldn't have missed that easy shot.

a. Yes, that's me.

b. I might do this.

c. I'd never do this.

5. Your gymnastics team lost the first three meets of the season. The most recent loss really hurt—you thought for sure you'd beat the Twisters. *If we didn't beat that team,* you think, *we're not going to beat anyone. This season will be awful.*

a. Yes, that's me.　　**b.** I might do this.　　**c.** I'd never do this.

Scoreboard

Lousy loser	Crossing the line	Winner's circle
If you answered **two or more a's,** you sometimes push blame onto other people and dwell on negative thoughts, and that doesn't help you or your team. Look ahead to your next game, and focus on what you can do to play your best.	If you answered **mostly b's,** you know in your heart what's right. Focusing on what teammates did wrong—or bursting the winner's bubble— may take away the sting a teensy bit, but it isn't OK. Neither is thinking negatively about your own performance! Follow your conscience.	If you answered **mostly c's,** you have the heart of a winner. Teammates who've made mistakes know what they've done wrong, so why make them feel worse? A loss is history—you can't change it. Sharing a positive attitude by being kind and encouraging raises everyone's spirits—and makes your team stronger.

I get distracted when I have to play against one of my friends. We go to different schools, so we compete against each other a couple times a year. How tough should I be on her? What if she gets mad?

Answer

Part of the fun of competition is testing yourself against the best your opponent has to offer. It won't feel like much of a game if both of you aren't giving your all. Doing your best no matter who your opponent is—that's what makes you true athletes.

Professional athletes often face friends on the field. Some are former teammates. Others are athletes they've come to respect and be friends with through years of competition. Do what they do. Before the game starts, go talk to your friend. Say hi, give her a hug, and say, "Play hard!"

During the game, if you're distracted by thoughts about your friend, treat the worry like any other "noise." Use it as a cue to remind yourself what you have to do in the game—like stay in position or look carefully before you pass the ball.

After the game, leave the analysis to the coaches. When you see your friend, congratulate her. Enjoy the fact that, win or lose, you both love to play. That's just another thing you have in common.

My dad loves basketball. I play—and so did my brother but he quit. Dad said that was OK, but he was really crushed. Now that I play in middle school, I don't like the competition and the time it takes. I want to quit, but I don't want to hurt my dad.

Answer

When sports are fun, they make you feel good about yourself—strong, capable, and in control. When they're not fun, they can make you feel weak or stressed. It's normal for there to be times when you ask yourself . . .

Is this the right sport for me?

Do I like playing at this level?

Am I having fun?

Is this a good fit?

Answer these questions and then, before you make a big decision like quitting, talk with your dad about your answers. Together you can look at what you used to like about basketball and also figure out what has changed.

Your dad may hope you keep playing because he knows sports can offer you so many brain, body, and life bonuses. Maybe you'll keep playing because you like being around friends or seeing yourself improve. Or you enjoy setting and reaching a goal. Find ways to get those good vibes flowing again—that's the best step to take before quitting.

87

The whole team is like a family, and you can trust them no matter what.
—Matti

Sports help me feel I belong.
—Kendyl

you &
the team

All sports are team sports, because you practice with other people and you work together to become better.

—Gwyneth

team sports or solo spirit?

There are *sooo* many fun fitness activities out there! One day a team sport may grab your attention. Another day, a solo activity may speak to your heart. There are lessons to be learned from both.

Teams come in lots of shapes and sizes.

In a high-speed game of hockey, it's pretty obvious everyone on the ice needs to work together to know (1) where the puck is and (2) how to get the puck into the opponent's net. The whole Arctics Hockey Club is a team, working together. At the same time, the three Arctics who skate onto the ice together as a *line*, moving the puck toward the goal—they are a mini-team.

You can be on a team and still be an individual.

A girl playing a singles tennis match can still be part of a team if she's playing for a club or school. And girls who play team sports still have their individual hopes, dreams, and styles.

Playing an individual sport doesn't make you less of a warrior.

A girl golfing with her cousin on vacation may be playing solo, but she's still focused on playing her best. And a competitive skateboarder wants to win, even if she's on her own in the bowl.

Even if you're solo, you're not alone.

At the dance studio, a girl may perform a solo and then dance in an ensemble 15 minutes later. A runner in the 1600-meter may feel alone on the track when her heart's pounding with three laps down and one still to go. But she's not—she may have a teammate in front of her and another behind her. That's a strength.

You have other teams in your life, too.

You may think, *I like solo sports the best*. You may prefer kayaking a quiet stream to a game of lacrosse, and that's terrific! The teams in *your* life are your family, French club on Wednesdays, your lunch buddies—any group that has a shared purpose and gives you a sense of belonging.

Teamwork lessons apply to everyone.

Knowing how to communicate, have fun, and problem-solve with people makes fitness a lot more fun. It also helps you in school and with friends and family, now and in the future.

you say

What's it like to play a sport where you're powered only by your own skills, spirit, and muscle?

How does it feel to play with the strength of all your teammates at your side?

Here's what athletes like you have to say.

With individual sports, you get to show your own skill.
—Jacqueline

I've made my three best friends ever from dance!
—Lydia

I like being on a team because if you don't win your own race, you have a whole team to help win the meet.
—Samantha

The cool thing about fencing is that it's both a team and an individual sport.
—Madilynr

I love the feeling when you've worked hard and contributed to your team's success.
—Sarah

I like sports that you can do alone but also with a friend.
—Maizy

I'd rather fly solo, because I can get things done and do them the way I want to.
—Caroline

I love being on a team, because it's like being part of a big family.
—CeCe

With team sports, if you're not good at something, your teammates can help you improve.
—Maddy

I love individual sports. I don't feel responsible for another person and no one else is responsible for me.
—Lily

all for one

You've seen the movie: The team is a bunch of misfits and newbies who bump into one another at every turn. Slowly they get better, and at the end—big hurray!—they bring home the trophy.

In real life, teammates don't go from chumps to champs in two hours. Teamwork takes time.

That happens at practices. Practices are a time to improve your skills, learn how to work with teammates, and get to know one another. The more comfortable you feel with your teammates, the easier it is to play as one smooth machine.

How well do you know your teammates? Look at the girl next to you at practice. Who's her favorite pro player? What's her dog's name? If you don't know, find out!

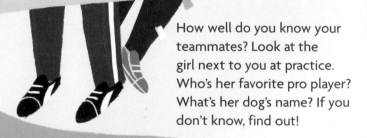

Once you and your teammates become friends, you develop a powerful closeness called *esprit de corps* (es-PREE deh KOR). It's the spirit that makes working hard fun and that binds you together *closerthanthis!*

Get-to-know-you games

To strengthen the bonds with your teammates,
play these games before practice, on the way to an
event, or even while you wait for your ride home.

Two truths and a tale

Stand in a circle. Each girl makes three statements about herself—two
that are true and one that's an untrue "tale." The girl to her left guesses
which statement is the tale. Then it's her turn. By the end, you'll know
much more about your teammates and their imaginations!

> I have a cat named Sandy Claws.

> My great-grandma played professional baseball.

> I rode in a submarine.

Fun facts

To play, you need a bag of colored items, such as large beads or candies.
Stand in a circle. Without explaining the rules, have each girl grab a hand-
ful from the bag. Surprise!—the number of beads or candies she grabs
equals the number of fun facts she has to share about herself. If you like,
make each color a different subject. For example:

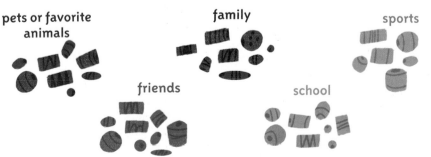

pets or favorite animals

family

sports

friends

school

95

got spirit?
let's hear it!

Here are ideas—big and small—for keeping your team's spirits high!

1. Decorate clear, lidded tumblers or reusable water bottles with the signature of every girl on the team, using markers in team colors. Or decorate with your team name and inspiring sayings. Drink up that team spirit!

2. Fill the time on long bus rides by making friendship bracelets in team colors.

3. Decorate plain cotton bags with nontoxic fabric paint in team colors. *Ta-da*—team totes!

4. Decorate the locker room with garlands before the big game. Purchase paper tassels or large pom-poms in your team colors from a craft store. With an adult's help, tie them to strings, and hang the garlands along the wall.

5. Make team hair ties to "tie your team together." Purchase narrow ribbons that use your team colors in a mix of stripes, solids, polka dots, and other prints. Cut the ribbons into pieces about 6 inches long, and tie several onto a ponytail holder.

6. As a team activity during holiday time, fill clear, ball-shaped tree ornaments with confetti, rolled paper, and ribbon in your team's colors. Make sure each girl gets a finished ball to take home. Have an adult help you hang the ornament in a fun place, such as in your window, on your bed frame, or on a tree limb—inside or out!

7. Decorate a round metal key-ring with strips of felt in team colors. Cut three ½-inch-wide strips about 9 inches long. Fold them in half around the ring, and wrap a narrow strip of colored duct tape at the top to secure. Add a tag that reads, "You're key to our success!" Share it with a team-mate whose spirits need lifting.

8. Make spirit shakers by filling clean, empty recyclable water bottles with colored plastic beads and ribbons in team colors. Label with your team name or mascot, and tie 8-inch lengths of colored ribbons around the cap.

9. As a good-luck gift, give a cute pair of socks with a note of encouragement or team spirit.

YOU'LL KNOCK THEIR SOCKS OFF!

10. Make a name pennant for a team member. Cut out a long triangle from colored felt. Use adhesive felt letters to spell out her name—and surprise her by taping it to her locker or door.

Craft smart

When making crafts, be sure to ask an adult before using any supplies, including markers, paints, glues, and scissors. Some supplies are not safe for kids, or they can damage surfaces. Also ask permission before using fabric or old clothing. And when you're not using them, keep all supplies out of the reach of little kids and pets.

JANE   LILY   JOJO

10 ways to be a leader

Teams are made up of all kinds of people: younger and older kids, speed demons and slow-but-steadies, girls with experience and girls with new passion. Everyone has something to contribute.

The best players know that being part of the team is more important than being the star of the show. They also know that the most talented athlete isn't the only leader on the team. There are other ways to show award-winning behavior. Challenge yourself—can you model at least five of these all-star actions at every practice?

Support

On the field, help other girls by sharing what you know—without making them feel dumb. If you notice a teammate is struggling with something off the field, such as a family or school matter, ask if she would like to talk.

Encourage

Praise other girls out loud—in front of the team—for things they do well. Prove that this is a team whose members support one another.

Make extra effort

Give it all you've got at practice, and truly pay attention to your coach. Always be ready to run one more lap.

Raise the bar

Challenge teammates in a fun and friendly way. If the coach yells, "Eight push-ups!" smile at the girl next to you and say, "I bet we can do ten. Let's try!"

Be a tough cookie

When you fall down, don't crumble. Bounce back up! If you make a mistake, move on instead of sweating it. Stay positive under pressure and mentally tough under stress. You'll empower others to do the same.

Be a storm chaser

Do you see black clouds of negativity forming? Take action! If teammates are complaining, focus on solutions instead of joining in. Show that "can't-do" attitudes have no place here.

Present with pride

Be a good representative of your team, your sport, and yourself. Be polite. Say please and thank you. Participate in class. Put down your phone and be interested in other people. Play with younger kids. Be someone others look up to—and someone *you* look up to!

Be smart

Show that academics matter. At weekend tourneys, don't be afraid to study in the hotel lobby. If the team has a long bus ride, crack open a book.

Connect

Make an effort to get to know *all* your teammates. Talk and share with the girls who aren't already your friends. Building relationships helps you care about one another. When you care, you work harder for each other in the game.

Energize

Keep the team's spirits high with a smile and enthusiasm. Both are infectious!

It's important to have your own goals, but remember—you need your team in order to reach those goals! You're in this together.

sounds like trouble

Teamwork doesn't always come easily. Know what bad behavior sounds like so you can turn your actions around. Stop trouble before it starts!

Responding to what the coach says with a moan or a groan sets a bad example—and puts a black cloud in your own brain.

Stating that something's impossible brings both you and your team-mates down.

Playing should be fun! But don't spend more time giggling than practicing.

You may want to be a coach someday, but you're not the boss yet! Leave the instructing to the person in charge.

It's right to let a teammate know you're wide open for a pass. But if you're saying "MINE!" too often, you may be too interested in being The Girl Who Makes The Big Play.

Keep your focus on playing well, not on having the hottest gear.

A grandstander is someone who does anything to get attention. And if your teammates are watching you, they can't keep their focus on the game.

Yo! That's a great song, but stop singing to yourself (or looking at the clouds). Keep your head in the game and your eyes on the ball.

coach talk

If you have a problem—say, you feel you don't get enough playing time—talk to your coach. She can't help you if you don't speak up! These tips make talking it out easier.

Coach first

Complaining to your teammates may make you feel better temporarily. But when griping gets back to the coach—and it always does!—it may make her less willing to hear you out later. Talk to the coach yourself instead of asking your teammates or parents to do it for you.

One-on-one

Approach the coach when she has time to think about what you're saying, not at a team meeting or in the middle of practice. Ask when she has time to discuss something important.

Calm rules

This isn't the time for tears or blowing your top. Speak calmly, and give an example that supports your point.

What not to say:

"I never get to swim relays! And I've been waiting for so long!"

Better:

"My times have really improved. I've been practicing my flip turns and exchanges. I'd like to try a relay so I can get more experience."

Final word

Even if you don't like your coach's answer, she's in charge. What she says, goes. But that doesn't mean you have to let go of your dreams! Set a goal for yourself, and break your goal down into baby steps. Think of at least two things you could work on to help you reach your goal by next season.

"But, Mom!"

If your mother or father coaches the team, you may get special attention—the good kind and the bad kind. Sometimes parents who coach give their daughters special favors. Other times they're extra hard on their own kids. Play it safe, and don't look for special treatment. Ask Mom or Dad to treat you as they treat the other players.

The moral of the story: Don't be afraid to talk to the coach if you have a concern. Tell her how you feel. The calmer and clearer you are, the easier it will be for the coach to help.

coaches' corner

Coaches can be friendly and funny, but tough, too. That's their job. Think of the best coach you've ever had. What made him or her great? The coach probably made you work hard but also made the work seem fun. With the coach's help, you discovered skills you didn't know you had.

A coach's job is to help you become a better athlete. So when a coach corrects you or gives you advice, don't take it as a personal insult. Coaches are there to teach you the rules of the game and help you develop the skills you need. That way, you're smart, strong, and ready to play when you take the field.

Too tough?

If your coach insults players or is mean or inappropriate in other ways, tell a parent. Ask your mom or dad to watch practice or a game and to evaluate the coach. If enough parents think there's a problem, they can talk to the school or the head of the league. Don't be afraid to speak up.

SPORTS Q&A

I love team sports, but I can't play right now. I need to be home after school to watch my little sister. My older brother has a job after school, so he can't help. I heard they might even cut back on recess at school! I miss my teammates and I miss playing.

Answer

There's an old saying that goes, "Find a way or make one." It sounds like you might do both!

Right now, family needs are your number one priority. Try using sports to bond with your sister. Teach her soccer or play games that get the two of you moving, such as tag or kickball.

At school, get a game of basketball or kickball going during lunchtime. Explain your situation to your PE teacher or principal. Ask if there are community groups that practice when you're free. Maybe you can start a morning running club with a teacher and recruit friends to join.

If you're upset that your school is cutting back on recess or sports, make your voice heard. Advocate for new sports, practice times, or recess to be added to your school programming. Find a way to be active daily, or make a way. You can do it. In the process, you'll become a sports advocate!

Help! It seems like only a few people on our team try very hard. Everyone else just complains about how we lose every game. What can I do?

Answer

When the whining is louder than the cheering, there's definitely a problem! It sounds like your team needs more players who lead by example—maybe you?

The key is to focus on what the team needs to play its best—and then lead the way with your actions. Leave the pep talks and discipline to the coaches. Instead, do your best during practice, and praise teammates who work hard. Point out when other girls make good plays, are in the right position, or execute what the coaches have asked.

If you consistently focus on the positive, other girls will follow. That should turn the volume on the whining way down.

Answer

Testing the rules has always been part of sports. There may be times when a coach instructs you to push the limits of what's legal. One example:

My coach showed us how to hold on to an opponent's jersey in a way that the refs can't see. Isn't that playing dirty? What do I do if the coach tells me to do something I don't think is right?

Sometimes soccer players fall to the ground when they aren't really hurt, trying to get a penalty called. While that pushes the rules, it does not break them. In many circles it's even considered normal.

But think about this. You could use a move on your opponent or be the fastest to the ball. Those are much more athletic ways to win the ball and create momentum for the team.

If you're ever confused or uncomfortable with anything your coach teaches, let your voice be heard! Tell the coach you're eager to learn ways to use your physical and technical skills to win balls and calls. Sometimes even adults need to be reminded that the rules are there to make the game fun—and fair—for all. Continue to test your own limits and play hard within the rules of the game.

Once I was playing soccer and a girl from the other team kept pinching me every time she was next to me. What should I do if I'm playing against someone who breaks the rules on purpose—or even with the blessing of her coach?

Answer

Playing hard within the boundaries of the rules is good. Some call that "being intense." But when those boundaries are crossed, it goes beyond intensity and into the zone of playing dirty.

Trying to win by pinching, kicking, or hitting your opponent is wrong. If the rules are broken repeatedly, bring it to the attention of your coach. State the facts: "Their forward pinched me three times" versus "There's a girl out there being mean." Hopefully, the coaches and refs can improve the player's on-field behavior.

But you can't control what either the coach or your opponent does. You *can* control what you focus on. Keep using your physical and mental skills—and strategy—to play your A game.

If your opponent plays dirty, it can actually be a sign that you're wearing her down. She's no longer using her skill to get an edge on you—she has resorted to pinching! Try smiling through these moments of dirty play. You'll send a strong message to the other girl that you know what she's up to, and you won't be distracted.

Ultimately, cheaters know what they are doing is wrong. They end up feeling bad about themselves. That means they lose the most in the end.

If you don't know what sport to do, just try one, and if you don't like that one, try something else. Your sport is up to YOU!
—Sadie

go for it!

you're a champ!

You did it! You crossed the finish line. The buzzer has sounded, but the fun is just beginning. Whether you play team sports or stay fit on your own, you're now stronger, smarter, and more sure of yourself than ever.

You've learned new skills and drills.

You know that when times get tough, you look a challenge in the eye and say, "Let's go."

Let's go.

You appreciate your body and all the amazing things it can do.

You recognize nerves and you aren't afraid of them.

I can do this. It's fun.

You know you can learn even more if you put your heart, mind, and body into it.

You know how to be a good teammate and a true leader.

Way to go, Priya!

You know everyone shines in her own way, on the field and off.

You know a good attitude is contagious.

You love your body and your whole self.

And in the big game of life, that makes you a champion.

Now and forever.

Go for it!

Got sports stories or fitness tips to share?

Send them to:
Editor, A *Smart Girl's Guide: Sports and Fitness*
American Girl
8400 Fairway Place
Middleton, WI 53562

All comments and suggestions received by American Girl may be used without compensation or acknowledgment. We're sorry, but photos can't be returned.

Here are some other American Girl books you might like:

Each sold separately. Find more books online at americangirl.com.

Parents, request a FREE catalog at **americangirl.com/catalog**.
Sign up at **americangirl.com/email** to receive the latest news and exclusive offers

Discover online games, quizzes, activities,
and more at americangirl.com